Philip and Rowena

A play

Gillian Plowman

Samuel French—London

CHARACTERS

Philip, aged 70
Rowena, aged 65
Janet, aged 30-40 years
Lilian, aged 70
Jeremy, aged 40
Heather, aged 37
Doctor

Time: The present
Setting: A hospice

Other plays by Gillian Plowman
published by Samuel French Ltd:

Beata Beatrix
Cecily
Close to Croydon
David's Birthday
The Janna Years
A Kind of Vesuvius
Me and My Friend
Tippers
Two Summers
Umjana Land

PHILIP AND ROWENA

The lounge of the hospice with an area for Rowena's room. Most props are already in situ. *Lighting is used to highlight other places, i.e., Heather's house*

The title music plays softly over the opening dialogue between Philip and Rowena

Philip and Rowena sit in adjacent chairs DSC. *Philip's is (not obviously) a wheelchair*

Philip We could be on a verandah overlooking the sea.
Rowena It's calm this evening. Look, the first twinkling light just going on.
Philip Must be a boat out there.
Rowena Or a mountain hut.
Philip What would you prefer? The mountains or the sea?
Rowena Mmm. Both? I haven't been here long.
Philip I know. You can have anything you like here.
Rowena I was very pleased to have tea with you — umm?
Philip Philip.
Rowena Rowena.
Philip My pleasure, Rowena.

The music and Lights fade

Rowena exits. Janet enters, wearing a Staff Nurse uniform

Philip puts on a beautiful waistcoat

Next morning

The Lights come up

Philip I don't want to see her!

Janet But, Philip, she's come especially ...

Philip I didn't ask her to. I've already got an appointment.

Janet With who?

Philip I don't wish to be rude, but it's no business of yours.

Janet Couldn't you see her whilst you're waiting for whoever it is you're seeing?

Philip No. She wants to talk about money and I don't.

Janet Philip. She's your wife ——

Philip No! Look, (*he hands her some money*) here's the taxi fare. Tell her to go home. Tell her to go wherever she wants, she has enough money.

Janet I think you're being most unreasonable.

Philip This is my time. I want it for myself.

Janet You must try and understand how she's feeling.

Philip Now that I'm leaving her? I understand all right. She's worried that she hasn't squeezed every last penny out of me. Well, I've sorted all that out. Tell her. She doesn't have to worry.

Janet She's worried about you.

Philip She doesn't need to. I'm enjoying myself.

Janet You want me to tell her that?

Philip We should have parted long ago. Best for both of us. I'm enjoying myself. Tell her that.

Janet She's feeling terrible, you know.

Philip She doesn't like me being here.

Janet You should talk to her.

Philip I haven't been able to do that for twenty years or more. Tried. Kept trying. Now I don't have to. Do I?

Janet I'll talk to her.

Philip You'll be kind to her. That'll be better.

Janet Do you want tea in your room?

Philip In the lounge please, Janet. A tray for two. By the window, please.

Janet (*muttering to herself as she goes*) In the lounge, please —
yes sir, no sir. Tea for two ... ?

*The Lights fade, then come up on Philip. Music is playing, the
window is open and there is the sound of birds outside*

Philip arranges the china on the tray

Rowena enters

Rowena Do you want to be on your own?
Philip No. I was waiting for you.
Rowena Were you really?
Philip Here. Sit here.
Rowena Thank you.

There is a small exclamation of pain as she sits

Philip All right?
Rowena Little twinge. Age, I'm afraid. Takes its toll.
Philip You're the most attractive woman I've ever met.
Rowena Me?
Philip And in the room right opposite mine. I can hardly believe it.
Rowena I was. I used to be quite a pretty girl. My daughter says
I'm "rather thin" now.
Philip Not thin, no. You can't see yourself. Your cheekbones are
perfect, eyebrows like bone china, and your eyes shine out
from under them, blue as the sky.
Rowena Should you be talking to me like this?
Philip I don't deserve to, do I? I'm a slob.
Rowena No, I didn't mean that ...
Philip Haven't looked after myself. If I'd known I was going to
meet you, I'd have taken better care.
Rowena I like that waistcoat.
Philip Do you? I brought it with me in case there was a special
occasion, and you see, there is. I know we only had tea together
for the first time yesterday, but you said you'd join me again

today and I've been so looking forward to it. To be honest, I've been up and down outside your room, waiting for you to come out. Did I miss you? Where have you been today?

There is a slight pause

Rowena Shopping. I wanted a new dress.

Philip I could have come with you! Why didn't you say? I'd have bought you a very beautiful dress. Did you go on your own?

Rowena My daughter picked me up. Heather. Conceived on the Isle of Skye. I hoped she'd be a free spirit but she's only happy in office blocks and taxis. Thinks she should run my life. But I gave her the slip. She was picking out some very dull dresses in Daley's and I just ran off and found the most beautiful dress shop. Silks and satins, swirls and flounces, you wouldn't believe ——

Philip I would, I would!

Rowena I tried them all on.

Philip And?

Rowena I couldn't decide! I couldn't. Am I too old for vivid red ?

Philip No, of course not!

Rowena And the purple was so pure ——

Philip Pure, yes! Like you!

Rowena —the blue was electric ——

Philip The blue, yes, that would — your eyes, you see. Yes, the blue! I'll buy you the blue.

Rowena You'll come with me and choose?

Philip This minute.

Rowena I'll try them all on for you to see.

Philip I'll buy you them all.

Rowena Oh, you dear man. But tea's this very minute.

Philip Wear the blue for dinner tonight. You'll have dinner with me tonight?

Janet enters with a plate of cake

Janet Philip's expecting someone so I've brought plenty of cake. What about you, Rowena? Are you on your own today?

Philip She's with me. We're fine, thank you. I'm not expecting anyone else.

Janet You're not ... ? But the cake ...?

Rowena What is it?

Janet Lemon sponge, I think.

Rowena Lovely. A slice, please, Janet.

Janet Rowena ...

Rowena Two slices.

Lilian enters, she has followed Janet into the room

Lilian What do you mean, you're not going to see me? Who the hell do you think you are? Giving your instructions. You're not in the factory now, you know. Not that you've been in the factory for half a bloody lifetime. Asbestos poisoning. Hah! I wish I'd had it. Then somebody might have given me a thought every now and then.

Janet Mrs Morley, I thought we'd agreed not to bother Philip today ...

Lilian I need to talk to him. There's two insurance policies I don't understand — I'm worried sick and all he can do is sit there with a very nice tea tray, thank you very much, and (*to Rowena*) excuse me, but I don't know who you are ...

Rowena I have the room opposite Philip's ——

Lilian Well, I hope he doesn't keep *you* awake with his snorting and his coughing — I tell you I haven't slept for weeks — what the hell are you wearing that for? It has to be dry-cleaned. I didn't pack that.

Rowena It's beautiful — I think — excuse me ...

Philip Don't go away.

Rowena I just want to get something from my room ...

Rowena gets up with a sharp intake of breath

Janet Can I get it for you?

Rowena No really, it's all right ...

Rowena goes to her room — out of the light

Lilian Don't some people's clothes hang on them?
Philip That's it. You're doing it again. Criticizing my friends. Most of yours sit on their fat arses, stuffing their faces, and contributing nothing except criticism to the world we live in.
Lilian So I've got a fat arse, have I?
Janet Mrs Morley, did you ring for a taxi?
Lilian No.
Philip All I know is that I keep spending money on clothes that are too small for you in no time at all. Now why is this? Do we deliberately buy stuff that shrinks?
Janet I'll go and do it for you. What about the insurance policies? Do you want to talk about those?
Philip No!

Janet exits

Lilian gets the insurance policies out

Lilian Philip, I'm going to see the solicitor in the morning. Just tell me which one of these is valid.
Philip They both are. Not only will you be free of me, but you'll be the richest woman around.
Lilian I've earned it. No-one can deny I've earned it.
Philip And I've earned some peace.
Lilian And what's all this about enjoying yourself? You're here for treatment.
Philip Listen. When the taxi driver takes you home, give him my best suit — the grey one — and ask him to bring it straight back, will you.
Lilian Your suit?
Philip I didn't bring it with me and I need it.
Lilian Nonsense. I packed everything on the list. You don't need a suit.
Philip And the tie that goes with it.

Lilian Which tie that goes with it?
Philip It's blue, it's just plain blue ——
Lilian You don't need a suit and tie — and I've thrown that old blue one away.
Philip Promise you'll send me a suit and tie or I'll tear these up.
Lilian It's gone to your head, Philip, you know that, don't you?

The Lights cross-fade to Heather's house

   Philip and Lilian exit

The phone rings in Heather's house. The front door slams

   Heather enters to answer the phone

Heather Coming. Coming. Hallo. (*She drops the phone*) God, sorry, dropped the phone. Hallo?

The Lights come up on Rowena who is on the phone in her room

Rowena Heather?
Heather Mum. I've just this second got in from work. Are you all right? Why are you ringing?
Rowena I want you to bring me something straight away.
Heather Oh, Mum, what? I was sure you had everything you needed.
Rowena It's my blue dress. The one with the beads. You know.
Heather No, I don't. Where is it? What do you want it for?
Rowena In the attic. In the brown trunk.
Heather In your house? Mum, that's miles away. I haven't time — in the attic?
Rowena Please, darling.
Heather Look, I can probably get it tomorrow. I'll bring it tomorrow.
Rowena I need it now.
Heather I wasn't going to see you today, was I? You wanted a time by yourself. Colin and I have a dinner date.

Rowena So have I. That's why I need the dress.

Heather You have a dinner date? Where? I mean, are you going out?

Rowena To dinner, yes. Thank you, darling, I knew I could rely on you.

Rowena puts the phone down

   The Lights fade on Heather, who exits

   Philip goes to Rowena's room

Philip Your tea's getting cold.

Rowena I had some of it. Do you want to come in?

Philip I'd like to see your room.

Philip manoeuvres his wheelchair in

   Park here, shall I?

Rowena Face the window. Such beautiful gardens.

Philip What happened to the sea and the mountains?

Rowena Different window! I had a cat once. Wouldn't go out the front door if it was raining. Always tried the back to see if it was raining there.

They laugh

Philip And was it?

Rowena Not to lose face, she pretended it wasn't and went out.

Philip Mine's green. My room.

Rowena I'll come and see.

Philip But this is nice. Did they give you a blue room because of your eyes?

Rowena You're mad about blue, aren't you?

Philip I'm mad about you. I wanted to send you all these flowers. I'm jealous of whoever sent you all these flowers.

Rowena My son and my daughter, that's all.

Philip Tell me about your son. I wanted a son. You have your own business and you want a son.

Rowena What business?

Philip Cabinet maker. Make anything for anybody so long as they wanted something special, because what I made was special. Little bit of me in those tables, those desks — and I wanted a son to teach him the ways of wood and craftsmanship. Wanted what I knew to go on, I suppose. Immortality is what we all want, isn't it?

Rowena Did you have daughters then?

Philip No children. Wasn't to be. Made us both selfish. Flourishing business, mind. Made a mint when I sold it. I can look after you, make no mistake.

Rowena But you must look after your wife.

There is a pause

Philip Yes, I know.

Rowena Jeremy, my son, is very protective. Protects his wife, his children and me. Very responsible chap. Very boring. I shouldn't say that, should I. My children aren't exciting.

Philip Say what you like to me. Say whatever you like. I'll never tell a soul. I'm devoted to you.

Rowena Since yesterday?

Philip If devotion started yesterday, it wasn't a minute too soon.

Rowena laughs

Rowena Fly me to the moon! I'd like to see the moon from the inside.

Philip No problem. We'll have dinner on the moon.

Philip sings "Blue Moon"

Rowena Oh no. Now the moon is blue.

Philip It always was, Rowena. It always was. I just didn't notice
before. (*But he is out of breath*)

The Lights crossfade

Janet and the Doctor enter the lounge area

The Lights come up on Janet and the Doctor

Janet Philip doesn't seem to have coughed so much today, but
he did become very distressed when his wife was here.
Doctor We need to help them to talk to each other, don't we?
Janet I don't think we're going to change the habits of half a
lifetime, Doctor. She's now convinced "it's gone to his head".
Doctor How far has he walked?
Janet He hasn't, I'm afraid. He's been in the wheelchair all day. I
think a stronger aperient is needed because of taking morphine.
Doctor Co-danthrusate ...
Janet Rowena took two slices of cake.
Doctor She didn't attempt to eat them?
Janet No. Just had them on her plate. I don't know what she was
trying to prove.
Doctor As a small boy in boarding school, a termly treat was
being taken to tea at Sadler's by Aunt Olivia. They had scrummy
fancy cakes. The anticipation and the pleasure of choosing it and
having it on my plate was far greater than the pleasure of
actually eating it. Though that was quite good, too ...

The Lights fade

The Doctor exits

The Lights come up on Philip and Rowena

Philip snores loudly. He wakes up and yawns

Philip I dropped off.

Rowena I did. But I woke up first and you looked very peaceful.
Philip Was I snoring?
Rowena No.
Philip Oh good.
Rowena I wouldn't mind if you did. I could close my eyes and
know that you were here.
Philip What was the most frightening experience of your life?

She thinks

Rowena Barricading the door against terrorists in Africa. My
husband was away; the children were little. I was pushing tables
and chairs but I couldn't move the sideboard. I thought, if I can
shove that against the door, they won't get in. I was yelling at
the kids to bring things and Heather wheeled her little doll's
pram along the hall. "That'll do it, Mummy," she said. They
broke the lock and the hinges, and the door and the furniture
and the doll's pram all started coming towards us.
Philip Oh Rowena, Rowena, I shouldn't have asked. What
happened?
Rowena Jeremy knew where Peter's army pistol was. He shot
them. All three of them. He was eight.
Philip What a brave boy.
Rowena Yes. I'm sorry I said he was boring. He just can't — risk
anything.
Philip Oh, my darling. Come here ...

Philip holds Rowena

Rowena Everybody said he was brave. He got a lot of attention.
But the doll's pram was wrecked and nobody noticed. Nobody
understood Heather's sacrifice. I didn't. Things went badly
wrong between Heather and Jeremy after that and I couldn't
put it right. They never see each other now. The last time was
at Peter's funeral. I would so love the three of us to be together,
just once.

Philip You will be.

Rowena The four of us.

Philip The four of us?

Rowena What's your most frightening experience?

Philip I've never had anyone to be frightened for. Never loved anyone. That's what's frightening. Living your whole life without loving anyone.

Rowena Your wife?

Philip Purely business. Her father wanted a partner, and I wanted a factory. She never forgave me for having asbestos poisoning when I married her. I think she felt it was grounds for annulment, because of my lungs. But the factory was in my name by then. So she stayed.

Rowena Your parents?

Philip Barnardo's boy, me. (*Slight pause*) Rowena, I'm not frightened any more ...

Rowena What?

Philip Now that I know what it's like ... to love someone.

The Lights cross-fade to Janet

Heather enters

Janet You look very nice.

Heather Supposed to be going out to dinner.

Janet Do you good.

Heather But I'm worried about Mum.

Janet She's fine. Taking a nap at the moment but I'm sure she'd like to see you all dressed up.

Heather No. I mean I won't disturb her. Um, what — what's she going to have?

Janet For supper? We're going to purée some fresh salmon. Do you think she'd like that?

Heather She's not going out to dinner?

Janet No. You're going out to dinner.

Heather She said she was.

Janet She'd probably like to.

Heather Yes. My father spoilt her, you know. Spoilt us all. We often ate out — the best restaurants. She hasn't been out much since he died. We should have taken her. I wish we'd taken her out more — before she had the tube.

Janet Feeling guilty, you know, is a very natural process.

Heather I always thought, there's plenty of time. I *will* take her out. No, it's not. It's not what I thought. I thought, why doesn't Jeremy come down and take her out. It's not fair. He doesn't, so I won't. It's like being kids again — "I've done the washing-up more times than you have." So stupid. I love her. Really I do.

Janet Well, find an opportunity to tell her.

Heather She wanted her blue dress. I didn't bring it. I didn't have time to get it.

Janet Let me tell you something. In the same way that fear requires imagination, guilt requires sensitivity. If a person hurts other people and has no intention of repairing the damage, or any desire to do so, then that person is unlikely to experience guilt. You're not like that. You have sensitivity, Heather. It's a positive quality. But it means you feel guilt as well.

Heather No, I haven't. I can't have. I would have noticed earlier. I'd have done something — I should have seen her more often.

Janet It wasn't your responsibility to *know*. There's no way of telling in the beginning. You mustn't blame yourself for that. Although you're not alone. Everybody does.

Heather Do they?

Janet Everybody thinks they could have done something to stop it. It's rarely the case.

Heather I don't know what I'd do if ...

Janet Look, come and kiss her good-night. Then go out and enjoy your dinner.

Heather I won't be able to. It doesn't make any difference to Jeremy, you know. He's in Paris on business. He doesn't care.

Janet He came to see her before he went and he's promised to bring her back some perfume.

Heather Typical, that is. Thinks he can make everything right with presents. Just like Father. Never gives her any time.

Janet You're angry, aren't you?
Heather Yes!
Janet I understand.

The Lights fade

Heather and Janet exit

The next day

The Lights come up on Philip in the lounge

Philip Good-morning.
Rowena Good-morning. I had a late bath. Luxury.
Philip Took my time myself. Well, we had such a late night.
Rowena Did we?
Philip Dancing till three.
Rowena Drinking till four.
Philip I was almost hungry again by the time I got to bed.
Rowena It was a lovely dinner, Philip. I did enjoy my ——
Philip What? What did you have?
Rowena *Coq au vin*? I love *coq au vin*. And *crême brulée*
finishing with the ooziest Brie I've ever squashed on to a biscuit.
Philip Good idea to go to Paris, wasn't it?
Rowena Yes. Did we both have *coq au vin*?
Philip Yes. — No, I had *bœuf bourguignon*. I knew I knew
something else French.
Rowena *Moules marinière*?
Philip Mmmm.
Rowena And the *Folies Bergère*? Did you enjoy that?
Philip Ummm ...
Rowena I didn't mind you looking at all those attractive girls,
you know. What energy they have.
Philip And so did we! I wasn't sure if you'd join in the can-can.
Rowena I wasn't sure if you would. Even after the can-can, you
looked immaculate in your — what were you wearing?
Philip My grey suit. Immaculately cut!

Rowena I was with the most handsome man in town.
Philip And you were wearing the blue dress?
Rowena With beads on.

Janet approaches with the drugs trolley

Janet Now then, Rowena, there's yours. And Philip, are you having
yours here as well? I shall need to make sure you've taken it.
Philip Where shall we go next?
Janet Nowhere until you've taken that.
Rowena Do you know, there's somewhere I've always dreamed
of going.
Janet (*to herself*) Staff Nurse Whelan, you seem to have
become an invisible person.
Philip Where? Rowena, where?
Rowena Florence! That's where I've always wanted to go!
Philip And me!

The Doctor approaches

Doctor Good-morning.
Janet Doctor, have you prescribed something for these two that
I know nothing about?
Doctor You're both pretty perky, aren't you? We'd better check
you out, but in your own rooms, please.
Rowena All those paintings. So much beauty will make me cry,
I know it will.
Philip I want a portrait of you, Rowena. We'll sit on the Uffizi
Palace steps, and some handsome Florentine will paint you in
the sunshine, whilst I watch ——
Janet And Doctor Mill, you too seem to have mastered the art
of invisibility.
Philip — and drink some wine.
Rowena From the great Tuscan vine! "Of the grapes they feed, of
the juice they make wine, of the shreddings they make firewood,
of the leaves they feed oxen, of the stones they feed pigeons."
Philip Waste not, want not.

Janet Ladies and gentlemen, this is the drugs trolley, not the
drinks trolley ——

Philip Not a second, not a minute, not an hour. I've had to
tell you everything straight away.

Rowena I know.

Philip Ask you everything straight away.

Rowena I know.

Philip Have I rushed things?

Rowena No.

Janet Of course, I don't have anyone else waiting anxiously for
me to reach them ——

Philip Ah, thank you.

Janet What for?

Philip The drinks.

Janet (*to the doctor*) Diamorphine '96.

Doctor Best brew around.

Janet And you won't feel a thing.

Philip Cheers.

Rowena giggles

Janet (*whispering*) Philip, Doctor wants to talk about your
bowels. Will you please go back to your room.

Philip Figs!

Rowena Fresh figs from Florence. Philip.

They laugh at the alliteration

Doctor Perhaps that's the answer, Janet. We'll get them both
some fresh figs.

Janet You're as bad as they are.

Doctor Is that what you meant, Philip?

Philip I want to pick them myself.

Rowena On a balmy evening ——

Doctor In the Boboli gardens.

Janet Where are they?

Philip
Rowena } (*together*) Florence!
Doctor

Janet I might have known. Well, I'm going to buy a handbag.

Rowena Where?

Janet Oh somewhere. In one of the shops. In Florence.

Rowena Let me come and help you. We'll buy some shoes to match. Oh, Italian shoes! Philip, we're going shopping again today.

Janet (*to the doctor*) Either I'm mad, you're mad or ——

Doctor (*to Janet*) Visualization.

Janet I know the theory.

Doctor Shutting out symptoms of pain and discomfort by bringing happy and relaxed pictures into the mind.

Janet and the Doctor move off, leaving Philip and Rowena in the lounge area

The sounds of street life in Florence

Rowena and Philip are on their feet and active in their other world

Rowena The buildings seem to be sunburned, don't they? Sunkissed. That lovely burnt ochre colour. We must have walked beautiful miles.

Philip Here's the straw market. Watch that scooter! Hold my arm, and don't let go.

Rowena I want a new hat.

Philip (*imitating an Italian vendor*) Signora, I have a thousand 'ats. The mosta beautiful for you. You try. Too big ... a. Too small ... a. Perrfectt.

Rowena It's lovely. Straw flowers and a silk lining. It's too expensive.

Philip Not for you.

Rowena (*as an Italian vendor*) And for you, Signor, a Florentine shirt. A work of art in itself, and so beguiling to the toucha, your lady, she will not be able to keep her hands off your shirt.

Philip It's orange!
Rowena Is it?
Philip The shirt.
Rowena It'll go wonderfully with your waistcoat.
Philip (*again as an Italian*) Now you musta toucha the nose of
   the famous lucky bronze bear.
Rowena Hallo famous lucky bronze bear. I'm touching his nose.
Philip Now make a wish.
Rowena Secretly?
Philip We haven't time for secrets.
Rowena I wish you would ask me to marry you.
Philip Will you marry me?
Rowena It came true! Thank you very much, famous lucky
   bronze bear.
Philip You've made me very happy.
Rowena I haven't given you an answer yet!
Philip Minx! You don't wear any rings.
Rowena Too big.
Philip Did Peter give you a sapphire?
Rowena No. A single diamond. I've given it to Heather.
Philip Can I buy you a sapphire? Blue ...

Rowena laughs

Rowena In the church of Santa Maria de Carmine, there's the
   saddest picture in the world.
Philip Do you want to go and see it?
Rowena Yes. Can we? I'll cry.
Philip Seems an odd thing to do when we're so happy.
Rowena Because with you I *can* cry.

A moment

   There.
Philip Expulsion of Adam and Eve from Earthly Paradise.
Rowena It's that absolute heartbreak on their faces. Her face —
   she has to go— I can't bear it.

Philip I know. I know.
Rowena Hold me ....

A moment

　Where next?

They spin around the room

Philip Turn left into the Piazza della Signoria where we can sit
　down and have a coffee.
Rowena Yes, I must sit down, I'm feeling very tired ... so tired ..

*Rowena sinks into a chair in the lounge, back in the real world. She
picks up a book on Florentine art which she drops as she falls asleep*

　Philip exits

　Jeremy enters, carrying a large bottle of perfume

Jeremy Mother? You dropped your book.
Rowena Mmm.

Jeremy picks up the book and reads the title

Jeremy Florentine painting.
Rowena Jeremy! What are you doing in Florence?
Jeremy Paris. — I brought you some *Je Reviens*.
Rowena Such a big bottle. I won't need all that.
Jeremy Of course you will.
Rowena Darling, it lasts for years.
Jeremy Can we go back to your room, Mother ——
Rowena It's very nice in the lounge.
Jeremy I want to talk — I need to talk to you privately ——
Rowena Where did Philip go?
Jeremy Philip? I don't know ....
Rowena He'll find me if I stay here.

The Doctor joins them, he brings a wheelchair

Doctor Hallo, Jeremy. Let's give you a hand to your room, Rowena.

Rowena You want to talk to me too? Well, I can't walk any more. My feet ache. I've trodden a hundred piazzas, you know.

Doctor Good thing I've got this very convenient wheelchair then. (*He takes her arm to lift her*) Up. Take her other arm like this, Jeremy.

Jeremy takes her other arm and they lift her

Good man.

They seat her in the wheelchair

And in.

They push the wheelchair to her room. The Lights come up on Rowena's room

Rowena Now then, what are we to talk about, Jeremy?

Jeremy I ...

Doctor He sees a difference in you.

Rowena Well, of course. I'm happy.

Jeremy How can you be happy? You're leaving us all. The children ...

Rowena I should like to see them. I'd like them to meet Philip.

Doctor Jeremy is frightened.

Rowena What of, darling?

Jeremy I don't know what to tell the children. I don't know whether to bring them.

Rowena Tell them that I've got a disease called cancer and that I'm going to die. I can't eat any more so I'm "rather thin", as their Auntie Heather would say, not that they ever see her which is a shame, Jeremy. But I'm having the most wonderful holiday here at the hospice, and if they want to come and see me, we could chat about what we think it will be like in heaven. They're bound to have some good ideas.

Jeremy starts to cry

Jeremy Oh, Mother ...

Rowena And tell them they can have a ride in my wheelchair. Philip will lend them his as well. They can have a race.

Doctor It's all right to cry, Jeremy. You're going to miss your mother, and she understands that.

Jeremy I love you, Mum.

Rowena I know, I know. I love you too.

Jeremy I feel so helpless. I want to do something.

Rowena I know. You want to look after me.

Jeremy Yes.

Rowena Like you always have done.

Jeremy No, I haven't.

Rowena You're a good son. And a good husband and father.

Jeremy Am I?

Rowena Jeremy?

Jeremy Yes.

Rowena See your sister. Just sometimes — see her.

Jeremy Yes.

They hold each other

And I want to know what the bloody hell is going on between you and this Philip!

Rowena laughs

Rowena Nothing. My dear boy, we're just good friends.

Jeremy I've heard that before! Well, I shall have to interview this young man. Find out his intentions. Is he good enough for you? What are his prospects?

Rowena (*laughing*) They're not very good actually. He's
terminally ill! Oh, Jeremy, you sound just like your
grandfather when Peter asked if he could marry me.

Jeremy Well, exactly. And I want to know if this — Philip's —
intentions are strictly honourable.

Rowena They're not. He fancies me.

Jeremy Outrageous!

Rowena And I fancy him.

Jeremy Hush your mouth! Did you know about this, Doctor?

Rowena All his fault! Jeremy, he stopped my pain. Those little
drinks that come round — stop the pain. Stop you worrying about
it coming back. I haven't been sick for a long time, and the ulcers
have gone from my mouth. My body isn't pulling me down any
more, so my mind is free, and it's having such adventures.

Jeremy I thought — I really thought you'd be sad and
frightened. (*He pauses slightly*) Because I am ...

Rowena Like you were in Africa? That brave little boy? You
saved my life then, Jeremy, and I'm still enjoying every
minute of it. Thank you for that.

They hug each other

Heather enters, carrying a blue dress

Heather I've brought your blue dress.

Heather and Jeremy look at each other

Rowena's face lights up

The Lights fade

Heather, Jeremy and the Doctor exit

Rowena changes into the blue dress

Philip and Lilian enter the lounge. Lilian   brings a bag containing Philip's grey suit and a new tie

The Lights come up on Philip and Lilian

Philip I want to ask you for a divorce.
Lilian A divorce?
Philip Yes.
Lilian Whatever for? We've managed all these years.
Philip Yes. Thank you for putting up with me. Everything's yours. Everything. I just want — a little freedom.
Lilian Does that mean you — don't want to come home again?
Philip Yes.
Lilian Janet explained.
Philip Did she.
Lilian I've brought your suit.
Philip Have you?
Lilian And I bought you a new tie to go with it. Try to remember to take the knot out when you've worn it. It'll last longer then.
Philip Yes, I will. It's all right about the divorce then?
Lilian Yes. It's a good idea. I won't be in for a few days. I'm going to stay with my sister. I'll sort it out when I get back.
Philip Have a nice time.

The Lights fade

Lilian exits

Philip changes into his suit

Music from Verdi's La Traviata *is playing*

The Lights come up on Rowena, looking beautiful in the blue dress, dancing round the room

Rowena All these grand people. "I'm with my husband", "We love the opera" — "Yes, we come to Florence every year", "It's like a second home to us", "No, thank you, he's bringing champagne. Nothing less than champagne, ever. He spoils me terribly".

Philip enters Rowena's room with two glasses

Philip I've never been to the opera before. Where is everybody going?

Rowena They're promenading. Showing off their outfits.

Philip Here's to you.

Rowena And to you.

Philip You look gorgeous.

Rowena So do you. I love that tie.

Philip Li ... (*he stops*) Thank you.

Rowena Let's join the giddy throng, and walk around admiring each other's outfits.

Philip Is that what we do?

Rowena In Florence, that's what we do.

Philip So what happened in the first act?

Rowena Violetta is a courtesan and likes to have parties. She meets Alfredo who has loved her from afar for a year. She has a slight cough which worries her, and she wonders idly what a new, calmer life with Alfredo would be like. However, she continues with the gay round of social pleasures.

Philip What happens next?

Rowena Well, he wins her over and they settle down together but his father thinks she is squandering Alfredo's money (which isn't true because she's selling *her* things to keep them in style) and that their union has brought shame on the family. So the father asks Violetta to leave Alfredo without telling him why, only they meet at a party again so she has to tell him she's in love with someone else (which she isn't) and he gets angry and shouts a lot. Then his father turns up and denounces his son's conduct because he's realised that he has wronged Violetta.

Philip Right.

Rowena   In the third act, she's very poor and ill with consumption. The lovers are re-united but it's too late for Alfredo to take her away. Re-living the joyful moments of their first love, Violetta dies.

Philip Load of tosh. I don't want to stay for all that.

Rowena Philistine.

Philip Come on, let's go.

Rowena Philip. We spent a lot of money on the tickets.

Philip Doesn't matter. Come on. Get on the back of my scooter.

Philip makes scooter noises

Rowena I'll ruin my dress.

Philip I'll buy you another. When are you going to answer my question.

Rowena Yes, of course I'll marry you. I've been pretending you're my husband already.

Philip Good. Because we're going to the Ponte Vecchio. Lots of people out this evening.

Rowena Don't mow anyone down!

Philip To the goldsmiths. To buy you the sapphire ring!

Rowena Oh, you dear man. Philip?

Philip What?

Rowena Being in Florence is like being in heaven, isn't it?

Philip Yes. Exactly that.

He makes more scooter noises

The Lights fade. Rowena goes to her room and gets into bed

La Traviata *is playing in the background. Otherwise, all is quiet*

Dim lighting

Janet, Jeremy and Heather enter

Janet meets Jeremy and Heather in the lounge area

Janet I'm glad you could both come — were both able to come.
   I won't be a minute.

Heather holds out her hand to Jeremy and he takes it

Janet moves to Rowena's room

Gentle Light

Rowena is lying in bed. Philip sits in his wheelchair near her

Janet I'll just come and draw the curtains, Philip. Getting dark.
Philip No. We're looking at the stars.
Rowena Dancing till three.
Philip Drinking till four.
Rowena What shall we do tomorrow?
Philip What would you like to do?
Rowena I'd like to go to the Uffizi Gallery.
Philip I'm not having you crying in front of any more paintings.
Rowena I promise. No more crying. And I'd like an Italian ice-
   cream.
Philip Yes. Ice-creams. We'll sit at that little table on the pavement
   in the Piazza della Signoria and watch the world go by ——
Janet She's asleep.
Philip She's not. We're talking.
Janet She's just dropped off, Philip.
Philip She mustn't do that. Rowena. What am I to do?
Janet You can keep talking to her gently. She'll hear you.
Philip I'd like to order two of your special ice-creams, please.

Heather and Jeremy move to Rowena's room

Janet Heather and Jeremy have come.
Jeremy Hallo, Philip.

Philip Four special ice-creams. It's about time you two showed up. We've been waiting ages. Heather and Jeremy are here, Rowena. Don't you ever keep your mother waiting like that again or you'll have me to contend with. Talk to her then. Now you're here.

Heather She's asleep.

Philip Talk to her! So that she knows you're both here.

Janet Philip — gently.

Philip I'm not getting angry. I'm not. I know what you want, Rowena, don't I ...

Janet Shall we go and get the ice-creams?

Philip I'm not leaving her — she wouldn't want me to go.

Heather No. Stay with us. It was a good idea of yours, Mum, for Jeremy and I to come together. He brought Sally and the kids over to our place and they're helping Colin get supper. They're lovely kids and we're all going to see lots of each other.

Jeremy I didn't realize, Mum — Imogen looks just like Heather. We got a photo out of when she was little — ever so alike.

Heather She hasn't got a doll's pram. We're going shopping tomorrow. I'm going to buy her one. Do you remember the one I had, Mum? I wonder what happened to it?

Jeremy And Joshua and Colin both support Chelsea. (*To Philip*) Football's not my thing.

Heather So they're off to the match on Saturday.

There is a pause

They all send their love. They wanted to come but ... (*She starts to break down*)

Jeremy They'll be mad about missing the ice-creams.

Heather It's nice, though, just being the three of us.

Philip Four of us. She wants it to be the four of us.

Heather The four of us. You smiled at me, Mum. She did, she smiled.

The Lights fade

Heather, Jeremy and Janet exit. Philip moves to the lounge area

The next morning

The birds are singing, early morning sounds can be heard

The Lights come up on Philip who is drinking a cup of tea. He is very breathless

Janet enters, wearing a coat

Janet Philip?
Philip Shouldn't you be off duty today?
Janet I am. I came in to see you. I'm so sorry, Philip.
Philip It's all right, Janet. We all stayed with her. She's gone back to Florence now. I'm planning to join her very soon. What are you going to do today?
Janet I'm going to buy some new shoes. Remember?
Philip Bring them to show me.
Janet Really? You want to see them?
Philip Next time you're on duty. Don't come in especially.

There is a pause

Janet You made her very happy, Philip.
Philip I know.

The Lights fade to Black-out

FURNITURE AND PROPERTY LIST

The multi-purpose set will facilitate some doubling of furniture. This is at the discretion of the director

On stage: **Philip**'s wheelchair
Chair
Window *By it*: table
Waistcoat
Two glasses
Tea tray with tea for two
Book on Florentine painting

HEATHER'S HOUSE
Front door (optional)
Telephone

ROWENA'S ROOM
Door (optional)
Bed
Window with curtains (optional)
Chair
Telephone
Vase of flowers

Off stage: Plate of lemon sponge cake (**Janet**)
Drugs trolley, with glasses (**Janet**)
Rowena's wheelchair (**Doctor**)
Blue dress (**Heather**)
Bag containing grey suit and tie (**Lilian**)

Personal: **Philip:** money for taxi
Lilian: insurance policies
Jeremy: large bottle of perfume

LIGHTING PLOT

Practical fittings required: nil

To open:	Lights up on Philip and Rowena	
Cue 1	**Philip:** "My pleasure, Rowena."	(Page 1)
	Fade to Black-out	
Cue 2	**Rowena** exits, **Janet** enters	(Page 1)
	Lights come up on Philip	
Cue 3	**Janet:** "Tea for two ...?"	(Page 3)
	Fade to Black-out, then lights come up on **Philip**	
Cue 4	**Lilian:** "... you know that, don't you?"	(Page 7)
	Cross-fade to **Heather**'s *house*	
Cue 5	**Heather:** "... Hallo?"	(Page 7)
	Lights come up on **Rowena**	
Cue 6	**Rowena** puts the phone down	(Page 8)
	Lights fade on **Heather**	
Cue 7	**Philip** "...didn't notice before."	(Page 10)
	Cross-fade to **Janet** *and the* **Doctor**	
Cue 8	**Doctor:** "... quite good, too ..."	(Page 10)
	Cross-fade to **Philip** *and* **Rowena**	
Cue 9	**Philip:** "... to love someone."	(Page 12)
	Cross-fade to **Janet**	

EFFECTS PLOT

Printed by
The Kingfisher Press, London NW10 6UG